TLC

TALKING AND LISTENING WITH CARE

*A Communication Guide
for Singles and Couples*

**Patricia Dixon, Ph.D.
Khalil Osiris, M.A.**

Oji Publications

TLC–Talking and Listening with Care:
A Communication Guide for Singles and Couples

Published by Oji Publications, a division of
Nuvo Development, Inc.
P.O. Box 372453
Decatur, GA 30037-2453

ISBN 0-9719004-8-5

To Anna Mae and Genie J. Dixon, Roman Blackwell
and Diane Parker

Patricia Dixon

To my sons, Adrian and Siddhartha with whom I hope to
always have great communication

Khalil Osiris

☥

The ankh was used in ancient Kemet (Egypt) at the time of passing to touch the lips of the deceased individual, to enable him or her to call forth the sacred breath or *word*, so that he or she could speak truth into eternity.

Acknowledgments

This book would not have been possible without the many relatives, friends, mentors, teachers, and leaders, who have inspired, encouraged, and helped us along the way. We are deeply indebted to the many ancestors whose backs we stand on. We would like to give special thanks to Maria Karunungan, an outstanding editor, Marsha Bonhart, and Justin Herman for their tremendous assistance.

Contents

Introduction

Communication is the most critical component of a relationship. If communication between two individuals is ineffective, it is highly likely that they will not be effective in their relationship. Although a lot has been written on interpersonal communication in general and African American communication in particular, few studies focus on communication for African American singles and couples. And there are even fewer studies, if any, that provide a practical guide for African Americans to communicate in a relationship partnership, with steps on how to resolve conflicts effectively. This is what *TLC – Talking and Listening with Care* provides.

Inspired by students who take the African American male-female relationships course at Georgia State University and the work we are doing with the African American Relationships Institute, *TLC* came out of the need for a communication tool that is centered in a perspective and crafted in a language that is culturally specific for African American singles and couples. It includes the African perspective on the spoken word, fundamentals for communicating effectively, gender differences, and African American communication styles.

TLC outlines three steps for communicating and provides a three–step program to help couples resolve conflicts. In addition, *TLC* includes exercises to help singles and couples examine their own communication styles, explore the source of these styles and to increase their communication competencies and skills. It is our hope that readers will be inspired by this work, and apply the principles outline throughout it, to their relationships.

The Power of Words

Thus said Ra, the Lord of all, Lord of the Utmost Limits, after he had come into being: I am the one who came into being as Kheper, *He who comes into being and brings into being.* All beings came into being after I came into being. Many were the beings that came forth from the *commands of my mouth.*

Selections from The Husia,
Maulana Karenga, 1989

The Word as Creative Power

Translated from one of the most ancient texts in Africa, these words speak not only to the creative power of the word but to how powerful words are. The creator creates himself and then goes on to create the world. We find this same story in the Judeo-Christian faith. Genesis 2 reads: "And the earth was without form and void; and darkness was upon the face of the deep. And the spirit of God moved upon the face of the waters. *And God said. . .*" And through spoken word, Jehovah goes on to create the world and everything in it, including human beings. In still another story of creation among the Fulani and

1

Bambara of West Africa, we find that God, or Maa Ngala, also creates humans by the spoken word. Amadou Hampaté Bâ (1981), in an article entitled, "The Living Tradition," explains how God creates Himself and then the world through spoken word.

> There was nothing except a Being.
> That Being was a living emptiness.
> Brooding potentially over contingent existences.
> Infinite Time was the abode of that One Being.
> The One Being gave himself the name Maa Ngala.
> Maa Ngala wished to be known.
> So he created Fan,
> a wondrous Egg with nine divisions,
> and into it he introduced the nine fundamental states of existence. (p. 169)

Bâ then goes on to explain that after the egg hatched, "it gave birth to twenty marvellous beings that made up the whole of the universe, the sum total of existing forces and possible knowledges" (p. 169). But God still was not happy with what He had created. So He went on to create human beings by first mixing the twenty existing creatures and then by "blowing a spark of His own fiery breath into the mixture. . .to whom He gave a part of his own name: Maa" (p. 169). This being, because he was named after God, and was given life through God's own breath, contained something of God Himself (p. 169).

Creation of Divine Speech

After creating Himself by first naming Himself, and then humanity, God invented speech as a means to communicate with humans. Bâ explains how this was done:

> Once Maa Ngala had created. . .Maa, he spoke to him and at the same time endowed him with the faculty of replying. A dialogue was begun between Maa Ngala, creator of all things and Maa. . . .As they came down from Maa Ngala towards man, words were divine. (p. 170)

Thus, because words came from God, and words were used by God to create humans and to communicate with them, speech is *a gift from God.*

Speech in Humans as Creative Power

Having been created in the divine image of God, human beings possess some of the same potentials as God. Like God they have the power to create through the use of speech. In fact, it is speech that puts everything into motion, even the divine potential in humans. And because God created the world through speech, then everything is speech in form. Bâ explains that, "everything in the universe speaks: everything is speech that has taken on body and shape. (p. 170)

Not only is everything speech in form, but speech also serves another function — that is to strengthen. It is taught in the Fulani tradition that "the Supreme Being conferred strength on Kiikala, the first man by speaking to him. 'It was talking with God that made Kiikala strong'"(p. 170).

But just as speech has the power to strengthen, it also has the power to weaken; just as speech has the power to create, it has the power to destroy. Thus speech can strengthen and it can weaken; it can create, and it can destroy.

Heart, Mind and Tongue

Karenga (1989) indicates that most ancient of our ancestors in Kemet taught the power of the heart, mind, and tongue, and the importance of their being in unison. In *Selections from the Husia*, he indicates that it was through the heart, mind, and tongue that God gave existence to all essences, to all living things: "Every word of God came into being through that which the heart and mind thought and the tongue commanded"(p. 6). God is therefore "within every body as *heart and mind* and within every mouth as *tongue*"(p. 6). Thus, "what the heart and mind think *and wish* is declared by the tongue" (p. 6).

Good Speech is Divine

Jacob Curruthers (1995) also teaches us how Good Speech is connected to Divine Speech. In *Divine Speech*, he informs us that "the proper designations of the deep thought of Ancient Kemet are *mdw ntr* 'Medew Netcher'(God Speech) and *mdw nfr*, 'Medew Nefer' (Good Speech)" (p. 39). However, there was no real distinction between Good Speech and God Speech. According to Curruthers, "Only Medew Nefer was in accord with Medew Netcher. . . .In fact, it is through the consistent practice of Medew Nefer, [Good Speech] that human beings finally attained Medew Netcher [God Speech]"(p. 40). Good Speech is therefore divine.

Towards Eternity

In ancient Kemetic or Egyptian thought, indeed in African thought, the goal of physical life is eternal life. How does one achieve this? One achieves eternal life through bringing good and doing good. Bringing good and doing good are in turn, achieved through words and deeds. Also, one must carry out his/her destiny or divine purpose. Our mates are therefore chosen to help us do good and bring good and to fulfill our divine purpose. However, to have a good relationship with someone, it is important to practice Good Speech. It is Good Speech that will help us have a relationship that is like heaven on earth. Indeed, it is the practice of Divine Speech that will get us to eternity in the afterlife.

Communication Fundamentals

Communication is a part of the human condition. Since we are interdependent and interconnected and have needs that can only be met by our connection with others, communication is necessary for our survival. How we communicate in interpersonal relationships will dictate the quality of those relationship. And the quality of those relationships will dictate the quality of our lives. Although there are many factors that could be focused on in interpersonal communication, some of the most fundamental include understanding the various kinds of talk and listening we engage in, how to talk and listen effectively, and how we process through our thoughts and feelings. Understanding gender differences in communication is also important. In addition, it is important to understand African American communication styles and how they can be used in constructive ways.

Talk

As indicated in chapter one, words are powerful. Whenever you talk, your words can be used to either strengthen the person you are talking to, or they can be used to weaken or break them down. When you communicate in a manner that strengthens and builds up, you are engaging in constructive communication. This is effective or good communication. Good communication not only strengthens your partner, but also strengthens you and your relationship. Communication that weakens or breaks down your partner is ineffective communication. Such communication can potentially destroy a relationship. Effective or good communication also depends on consistency between the components of communication or talk. There are two types of talk that generally occur. These are internal or *Inner Talk* and the other is external or *Outer Talk.*

■ *Inner Talk* is the internal conversations that occur. As Curruthers (1995) explains, "One thinks in speech. Even when one only 'thinks' about thinking, one thinks through (silent) speech" (p. 44). There are two types of internal talk:

● *Heart Talk*—The heart is the innermost part of our being and is the center of our emotions. It therefore speaks to our feelings. It is the heart that tells us what we are feeling.

● *Mind Talk*—The mind is the center of our thoughts and perceptions. The mind tells us how we are perceiving and what we are thinking.

Although heart talk speaks to how we are feeling, as with mind talk, we only understand these feelings through words. Inner Talk leads to Outer Talk.

■ *Outer Talk* is external expression that reflects inner talk. There are two types of outer talk:

   ● *Word Talk* is the verbal content of external expression. It is the actual words we use.

   ● *Body Talk* is how we use the body to express what we are saying. Body talk includes how we use our voice, facial expressions, gestures, hand movements and body posture, position, and orientation.

Although it can be argued that the body cannot talk because talk is utterance, articulation of words, the authors argue differently. As indicated previously, Bâ (1981) points out that, from an African perspective, "everything is speech that has taken body and shape" (p. 170). We therefore, also speak through usage of our bodies. Body expression is a reflection of inner talk, taking shape and form. Therefore, since bodies articulate inner talk, our bodies talk.

Figure 1

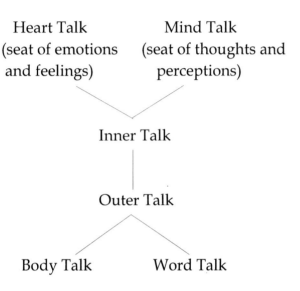

Heart Talk
(seat of emotions
and feelings)

Mind Talk
(seat of thoughts and
perceptions)

Inner Talk

Outer Talk

Body Talk

Word Talk

■ *Spirit Behind Words*—Important to note is the spirit behind the outer expressions. In the African world, it is understood that nothing happens outside of spirit. Every action has a spirit behind it. The spirit of the message has to do with motivation or intent behind body and word talk or verbal and nonverbal expressions. Every outer expression is a reflection of spirit or intention. What you should ask yourself is what is the motive or intention behind the words I am speaking?

Overall, when you send a message, this message consists of three components: spirit, which gives off energy or vibrations; word talk — what you say, your actual verbal expressions; and body talk — how you say it, your nonverbal expressions.

Words for Thought

- We listen with our eyes. That is we typically pay more attention to body talk than to word talk. Body talk, therefore, carries more weight. Research has found that how you talk rather than what you say carries about 65 percent of the message.

- The spirit behind what you say has great impact. People can detect energy and vibrations and may respond to this more than to what you say.

- We all have a unique way in which we communicate. Some of us are passionate and dramatic when we speak, using a lot of space and large hand movements. Others are quiet speakers, who use very little space with little or no hand movements. Some of us are primarily inner talkers and do not have much to say at all, while others are outer talkers and have a lot to say.

- Word talk is irreversible. Once spoken, words cannot be taken back, changed or undone. It is, therefore, important to think about what you are going to say before you say it.

- Words can wound a person for life. If it is true that we will be held accountable for all words and deeds, the words you speak can hurt you for eternity.

Talking and Listening

Words take on significance based on the meanings we attach to them. Communication between two people means that at different points one person will be talking and the other will be listening. The talker is the person sending the message and the listener is the person receiving the message. Interpersonal communication is effective to the extent that (a) the talker talks in a way or uses language that is constructive, and (b) there is consistency between the various components of talk. A message is also effective to the extent that the listener receives the message as was intended by the talker.

Figure 2

Talker - Use words that are constructive - Shows consistency between word talk and body talk	Listener - Interprets the message as intended

- Effective talking depends on

  - how the message is sent by the talker, which depends on the use of constructive words and consistency between word talk and body talk.

- Effective listening depends on

  - how the message is received by the listener, which depends on how accurately the listener interprets the intended message.

Ineffective Talking

An ineffective message may consist of word or body talk that is destructive. A message is also ineffective if there is inconsistency between word talk and body talk. For example, a person may be saying one thing from their mouth, but their body talk indicates that inner talk, either mind talk or heart talk—is different.

- *Destructive Word Talk* undermines the personhood of the listener in some way. Such words have the effect of hurting, wounding, and ultimately destroying relationships. Examples of destructive word talk are:

  - Attacking by name calling, belittling, criticizing, or judging

  - Blaming/Accusing a person of something

  - Questioning a person's trustworthiness or credibility

  - Disapproving of, or showing contempt or disgust for the person

  - Commanding, demanding or attempting to boss a person around

■ *Destructive Body Talk* includes facial expressions, gestures, body orientation and posture, and usage of the voice in ways that show indication of what is listed as destructive word talk.

● Facial expressions — frowning, looking disgusted, avoiding eye contact.

● Gestures — pointing fingers, moving the arms in a large jerk-like fashion, moving the head and neck in a side-to-side motion like you are telling someone off.

● Body — orienting the body away from the person as if you are not paying attention, standing in a way that indicates that you don't care, holding your hands on the hips, jumping up and down while yelling, approaching a person in a threatening way.

● Voice — volume, speed, tone, and pitch that give negative vibrations and sounds negative to the listener.

Ineffective Listening

How the listener receives a message is determined by his/her attitudes and beliefs; whether he/she thinks the talker is trustworthy or credible; his/her perceptions, which may be affected by his/her past and present experiences in general and with the talker; and his/her needs, wants, goals and expectations. If the listener is having negative thoughts or feelings on any of these dimensions, it may diminish his/her ability to listen effectively.

Effective Talking

Talking effectively means avoiding the types of word and body talk listed previously. It means communicating in ways that show that you believe your partner is worthy of your consideration and respect and that your word and body talk are consistent.

Effective Listening

Listening effectively means communicating that you are listening and want to do so with care and understanding. A major strategy for effective listening is to indicate that you have heard your partner and understand what he/she has said.

Effective talking and listening are expanded on in the chapters focusing on Talking and Listening with Care — TLC. However, to engage in effective talking and listening, it is important to understand some of the reasons that we communicate.

Communication and Connection

Although there are many reasons for communication, an underlying purpose for communicating in interpersonal relationships is for the individuals to connect with each other. There are two types of connection each requiring certain talking and listening skills. These two types of connection are being referred to as surface-level connection and deep-level connection.

■ *Surface-Level Connection* is the kind of connection we have with co-workers, acquaintances, and other associates. Much of the talk is surface-level, which may or may not impact us deeply. In places of employment, the connection might have to do with power relationships, which in turn depends on the amount of power an individual has over one due to the need to maintain one's employment, and therefore, one's income and lifestyle. The relationships here are established as subordinate or superordinate, and this dictates the kind of relationship and kind of communication. The individuals may otherwise have no interest in getting to know one another but wish to be cordial, or have a good working relationship without having to be interpersonally or deeply connected. When individuals get to know each other on a deeper level, they have a deep-level connection.

■ *Deep-Level Connection* is the connection between relatives, friends, and intimate others. Individuals can be effected more by the communication because they are deeply connected.

Just as our connection is surface or deep, so too is communication designed to connect on surface and deep levels. The type of talking will dictate the type of listening that is required.

When we engage in conversation, we are engaging in different kinds of talking and listening. Although the types of talking and listening can be classified in many ways, we are classifying them as follows: (a) functioning, (b) sharing (thoughts/experiences), (c) problem solving, and (d) exchanging ideas.

As indicated in *Table 1,* the first two types of communication (functioning and sharing) can be engaged on both surface and deep levels. For example, functioning communication may only require surface listening. It may require deep listening to the extent of the details involved. Also, if there is conflict over roles, or role expectations, then this would require deep talking and listening to resolve the problem. If there is sharing of thoughts and feelings, the listening would be deep or surface, depending upon what is being shared and how much the individual talking needs the focus of the listener. For example, if your partner is just sharing the events of the day, expressing his/her thoughts and feelings about something, but do not need your active participation, deep listening would not be required. However, if he/she is sharing something he/she feels deeply about and needs your attention, then deep listening would be required.

When your partner is disclosing past or present experiences that caused him/her to feel deeply, not only may he/she need your undivided attention, he/she may also need you to show that you care and understand. Talking to someone who shows care and understanding of things that have caused one pain, as well being able to share things that have caused feelings of shame and being able to share secrets, can increase one's feeling for the person. Being able to disclose oneself without being judged or criticized can make one feel more connected to the individual, increase intimacy and increase the overall quality of the relationship.

Table 1

Type of Connection Type of Communication	Examples of Surface-Level Talking/Listening	Deep- Level Talking/Listening
Functioning **Informational** **Instructional**	 "The plumber will be coming today." "Next time the alarm goes off, just put in the code."	Deep to the extent of details involved. Also deepens if there is conflict around issues like role expectations.
Sharing **Experiences** **Feelings** **Thoughts**	 "My day at work didn't go so well" "I don't think I like my job anymore." "I was thinking maybe I should consider looking for another job."	Deep if individuals are sharing information that they need their partner's help on. Also deep if one partner is disclosing or sharing past or present experiences that caused deep feelings. Increases intimacy and relationship quality.
Problem - Solving **Individual** **Couple**		 Requires listening, caring and understanding Requires talking and listening with care

Exchanging Ideas		Might consist of views around politics, religion, the African American global struggle; expansive in that it helps individuals to grow. Also undergirded by world view and values.

Exchanging ideas is another form of deep-level communication. It may involve discussions around issues other than the relationship. As with sharing or disclosing thoughts and feelings that are deeply felt, exchanging ideas may expand a person's view of the world and help individuals connect at a higher level. This level of communication is expansive to the extent that the individuals share the same world view and values, and to the extent that each can help the other grow. It is important to be able to communicate effectively and consistently at lower levels, in order to reach a point where there is more communication at higher levels.

When you and your partner are able to communicate at higher levels, it deepens your connection, making you feel like one.

Processing Styles

Some people experience the world more inwardly, have a more inner orientation, or are more introverted. Others, on the other hand, experience the world more outwardly, are more outwardly oriented and are more extroverted. Because we have different ways in which we experience the world, we also have different ways in which we process thoughts and feelings. People can therefore be categorized as *Inner Processors* and *Outer Processors*. There are also *Avoiders*, those who avoid dealing with their thoughts and feelings.

- *Inner Processors* are individuals who need to work through their thoughts and feelings first before talking about what they are experiencing. In some instances the person may distance him/herself until he/she works through the problem. After he/she has finished processing his/her thoughts and feelings, he/she is then ready to talk. If you find that you are with someone who is an inner processor, you may need to give him/her the space he/she needs to work things out. Equally, important is that if you are an inner processor you need to communicate in a positive way to your partner that you need time to think about things, and that you will be available to talk once you are finished working through your thoughts and feelings.

- *Outer Processors* are individuals who need to talk about their thoughts and feelings as they work through problems. Individuals like this may talk to their partner, relatives or friends until they feel that they are comfortable with how they feel about what they are experiencing. When a person is an outer processor they may have to discuss an issue or problem immediately. They cannot move on, rest or sleep until they have talked about the problem. If you are an outer processor and have a problem that involves your partner, it is still important to consider the factors outlined in our TLC Three-Step program in chapter five, which includes taking into consideration timing, what your partner may be going through, and how discussing the problem with your partner or others will affect your him or her.

- *Avoiders* are people who do not deal with problems at all — internally or externally. Because working through their thoughts and especially their feelings might open wounds, cause them to have to deal with themselves and/or the other person, they may avoid problems altogether.

Avoiders might also be in denial about realities and/or might just be irresponsible and assume the role of a child in the relationship.

Gender Differences

The popular works of Deborah Tannen (1990), *You Just Don't Understand* and John Gray (1992), *Men are from Mars and Women are from Venus,* provide insight into gender differences in communication. In these works these authors describe the sources of gender differences, the values underlying them, and some of the behaviors. As shown in *Table 2,* according to Tannen (1990), much of the style of communication of males and females begins with early socialization, which stems primarily from play and interaction.

Although they often play together, boys and girls typically play in same-sex groups. This means that the games they play and the language they use are different. *As shown in Table 2,* Boys typically play in large groups with a hierarchy, an elaborate system of rules, and a group leader who gives orders. For boys, the game itself is the priority. The play is competitive; it has winners and losers, and is based on status, which has to do with who is more skilled or best at what.

Girls, on the other hand, typically play in small groups or pairs, where friendship, being liked, and closeness are key. It is not about who is better at what. Girls' games, for example, hopscotch and jumping rope, are more focused on making sure everybody gets a turn.

With regard to communication, a way to achieve status for boys is to be the center of focus by telling stories or jokes or by challenging others. (For many African American boys it may be in the form of signifying or playing the dozens, which is discussed next). For girls, communication may not be about being center stage, or jockeying for status. It may be about sitting together and talking. Also, boys and girls have different toys. For example, girls have dolls and house toys, such as kitchen centers, emphasizing domestics and nurturing; whereas boys' toys emphasize competitiveness and aggression, for example sports toys and guns.

These early forms of play emerge in the values that men and women eventually adopt, what is important to communicate about and how they do so. Although relationships are important for men, status, skills, and competency tend to be valued even more. Although status and being skilled and competent may be important for women, relationships tend to be more highly valued.

For women the primary goals of communication are to maintain closeness and connections, to preserve intimacy, and to avoid isolation and being pushed away. The motivation for men in communication is to maintain their status in what is perceived as a hierarchy and to maintain the upper hand in order to not be put down or pushed around. The motivation is also to preserve independence, to not be bossed around.

Table 2

	Boys/Men	Girls/Women
Socialization Early play	Competitive — large groups with rules, focused on status, and who is best at what	Sharing — small groups/pairs, based on friendship, being liked and closeness
Values	Skills/competency, status, independence	Relationships, connections
Communication Motivation	To maintain position in hierarchy; to preserve independence; to avoid being pushed around	To maintain closeness; preserve intimacy; avoid being isolated or pushed away
Communication Styles	*Report* talk — do better in public conversation where they hold center stage	*Rapport* talk — do better in private conversation where they don't have to worry about being judged

A major difference in communication styles for men and women, according to Tannen (1990) is that for men communication is *report* talk while for women it is *rapport* talk. Many men, therefore, do better in public conversation in which they are the center of focus. Women spend a lot of time talking about their thoughts and feelings. It is a way to build rapport and therefore maintain closeness. They, therefore, generally do better in private conversation. Also, women generally do not like to engage in public conversation where they can be judged by others. Again, both of these communication styles stem from early socialization. Women usually had a best friend with whom they talked to about everything and with whom they felt close. As adults for some women, there is still the need to talk about everything as a way to share and feel close. For men, on the other hand, in order to maintain status in a world that is perceived as being hierarchal, it is important to hold center stage, which is achieved by exhibiting knowledge and skills, or verbally performing through storytelling, joking, imparting information, or lifting and transforming (as ministers and motivational speakers).

Another difference is what men and women communicate about. Since women are more private-talk focused, and their socialization as girls was usually a best friend, someone with whom they shared their secrets, the details of their day, and their fleeting thoughts, they are used to talking about these kinds of things. For men, the details of their day and their fleeting thoughts and secrets may seem unimportant. This may be why many men do not talk about these kinds of things, and why they do not understand what women want from them when they do talk about them. Because men use communication to preserve independence and to avoid being pushed around, they may see women who seek intimacy through talking all the time as trying to manipulate them or control their independence and freedom.

Another major difference in communication between men and women is how they process their thoughts and feelings under stress. John Gray (1992) asserts that women generally cope with stress by talking about problems, while men cope with stress by going inward. A major reason men cope with stress inwardly is because of the importance of being competent. Because masculinity includes being competent, men feel compelled to be problem-solvers. When a problem arises men may feel that they are supposed to be able to solve it. If they cannot, then they may feel incompetent. Therefore, they generally will not talk about a problem until they have found a way to solve it. This leads them to go inward to work through their thoughts and feelings until they have found a solution. It may only be after they have found a solution to a problem that they feel comfortable talking about it.

Women, on the other hand, are not under the same pressure as men to be problem-solvers. They do not have to show that they are competent to be feminine.

Women typically need to talk to work through their thoughts and feelings while problem-solving. Talking through problems helps women to work through their feelings and is something they may be more adept at since they have been doing this since childhood.

Many men are not adept at talking about their emotions or feelings. Thus, if a problem or issue arises that requires them to have to deal with their emotions, since it is supposedly unmasculine for men to be emotional, this may inhibit communication. Other men may completely shut down. Also, because of physiological differences that trigger the fight or flight response, if the communication is too intense, some men may feel the need to act out their emotions through physical violence. The other alternative is to flee, which means blocking out or exiting the scene. If a problem persists over time, men may seek to emotionally distance themselves in order to cope.

Overall, because men and women often do not know their different motivations for communicating and differences in communication styles, this can sometimes lead to communication break-down and unnecessary power struggles. It is, therefore, important to pay attention to gender differences in communication to sustain a healthy relationship.

African American Communication Styles

Molefi Asante (1987), in *The Afrocentric Idea*, informs us that African American communication is linked to the oral tradition in African culture. Since it is understood among Africans that *Nommo*, or spoken words can create, transform and strengthen, it is those who are gifted with verbal ability who are highly regarded. Like Africans, African Americans know intuitively the transforming power of words, which is why those who are gifted with verbal ability are also accorded high status. African Americans also have unique ways in which they communicate. These ways of communicating are used in every-day talk as well as in conflict, often without the speaker's awareness that they are being used. However, if used with conscious intent, these practices and styles can be used more constructively in conflict.

Thurmon Garner (1998), in an article entitled *"Understanding Oral Rhetorical Practices in African American Cultural Relationships,"* points out that, communication for African Americans is characterized by several unique practices. Some of the practices include indirection, inventiveness and improvisation, and playfully toned behavior.

Indirection involves communication that meanders around the point through asides or stories. It uses "innuendos, insinuations, inferences, implication and suggestions to make a point" (p. 31). It involves the use of circumlocution or coming to the point in a circular manner. Because it is undergirded by the philosophy that it is not good to put others on the spot, its explicit or implicit content can also be used to avoid conflict. Thus, one of the major strengths in this communication practice is its use in reducing or avoiding conflict.

Improvisation and inventiveness are characterized by spontaneity in the creation and use of communication. "Invention is creating new ways of saying the same thing, while improvisation is taking a message and manipulating it in new directions" (p. 32). A major focus of improvisation and inventiveness is the way it invites or challenges the listener's or participant's personhood. Essentially, the 'listener/participant is skillfully challenged to accurate interpretation, to discover hidden meaning which calls forth his personhood' (p. 33).

Playfully toned behavior or play "is a non-serious, sometimes, non-threatening, verbal exchange. It's a symbolic exchange of selves, and entertainment of each by the other" (p. 33). One critical aspect of this type of communication is that it is often left to the listener to determine if what is said is "serious" or "play." One benefit of verbal play is that in the event of confrontation, "the use of playfulness can often quell emotionally charged conflicts"(p. 52).

Garner (1998) also identifies several communication styles among African Americans. These include playing the dozens, rapping, boasting, and signifying. All of these styles are characterized to some degree or other by indirection, inventiveness and improvisation, and playfully toned behavior. Although these communication styles are used unconsciously among African Americans, they can be used consciously and constructively to de-escalate conflict.

De-escalating Strategies

■ *Playing the Dozens*, also referred to as "joaning," is a form of verbal aggression that may or may not make use of obscene language. It is essentially a verbal fight where the central focus is "cracking on" or putting down the opponent's mother. It functions as a release for African Americans of the hostility they experience due to oppression. For African American males, it is a mechanism to help them move away from identification with their mothers. It also helps them learn self control — that is, withstanding put-downs without physical aggression demonstrates strength. Because it is also a form of play, and is used to mitigate conflict, playing the dozens can also be seen as a form of conflict resolution for couples. For example, in the middle of a potential conflict, one could interject out of nowhere:

Oh, you just mad cuz yo' momma is... (<u>Note: the statement would be something that is not true</u>).

- *Signifying*, also regarded as "cracking," is the "verbal art of insult." It is talk in which the talker humorously puts downs, talks about, or makes fun of a person. As a form of play, it can also be used to tell somebody about him/herself, "put somebody in check," or "make them think about" or "check their behavior" (p. 39). Because it relies on indirection and talking in a circular direction, the meaning of the words is often hidden and implied. Thus, one can say one thing and mean something else. Signifying or cracking, because of its humorous nature, can also be used to de-escalate conflict. For example, in the midst of a conflict, one of the partners in an attempt to de-escalate might ask:

Why yo' head so big?

- *Rapping* is essentially romantic talk from an African American man to an African American woman in an effort to win her affection. It is a socially accepted way for a man to initiate conversation with a woman with the aim of a possible relationship. Although Garner (1998) indicates that it is not a conflict resolution strategy, we would argue to the contrary. For example, when verbal exchange is becoming emotionally charged, in order to de-escalate, the male and in some instances the female may begin to "*sweet talk*" the person or go into a rap mode to lighten the conflict:

> "*Why you being like that baby? You know I wouldn't do anything to hurt you. You know I luvs you.*"

■ *Boasting* is a humorous way of praising oneself for one's superiority over others. It is an exaggeration of one's strengths or abilities. A person may boast of topics "such as physical strength, personal appearance, personal accomplishments, and economic well–being"(p. 38). Essentially, the individual may build an image "through the sheer power of words" (p. 83). Boasting, because of its humorous nature and form of play, can also be used in tense situations to help de-escalate conflict. For example, when a situation is escalating, one of the parties might interject by saying:

"You just playa hatin.'"
"You just mad cuz I'm a bad Mama Jama."
"You can't talk to me like that cuz I'm big daddy."

Overall, playing the dozens, signifying, rapping and boasting are unique communication styles to be valued. They rely on practices that communicate with a great deal of ingenuity. Many African Americans are gifted in how they use words. Unfortunately, the gift of word usage, can exacerbate conflict if words are used in ways that hurt, wound, or undermine an individual's personhood. An understanding of and appreciation for our styles of communication is therefore important. It is also important to understand how these styles of communication, if used constructively, can help to de-escalate and reduce conflict and lead to more effective communication. Effective communication is good communication, and good communication can help to sustain a quality relationship.

In summary, effective communication is essential for a quality relationship and a quality life. In order to communicate effectively, it is important to understand the components of communication. Talk consists of inner talk and outer talk. Inner talk consists of heart and mind talk. Outer talk consist of word and body talk. Effective communication requires that inner talk and outer talk be consistent. It also requires that word talk and body talk are consistent and that the words used are constructive.

Effective listening requires interpreting a message without putting oneself in it, particularly if it leads to interpreting the message in a negative manner. It is important to know that the point of communication in interpersonal relationships is for the individuals involved to connect. This requires the listener to pay attention to discern the intent of the talker, to determine if listening should be surface-level listening or deep-level listening. On deeper levels, the listener must use care and understanding. Individuals have different ways in which they process their thoughts and feelings, and it is important to know the processing style of your partner and your own. What can also help in understanding communication styles is to understand gender differences. Also, African Americans have unique communication styles, and if used constructively, these styles can be used to help de-escalate conflict. Now, let's turn to talking and listening with care—TLC.

Talking and Listening with Care–TLC

Talking and listening with care consist primarily of three components: (1) talking, (2) listening, and (3) caring. TLC is the merging of the three components: effective talking and listening with a caring attitude.

A Caring Attitude

In communicating, our attitude reflects our perceptions of and how we feel about the person with whom we are communicating. It reflects whether we think they are important, and whether their position or opinion about a matter counts. We can adopt one of two attitudes:

"You are not a person of worth — your thoughts and feelings are not important to me." This can translate into *"I don't care about you."*

Or

"Being created in the divine image of God, you are worthy. I honor and respect you and therefore value your thoughts and feelings." This can translate into an attitude of *"I do care about you."*

Our attitudes may be influenced by past experiences with others, including caregivers, friends, and intimate partners. Since words can create or destroy, what we say can have a boomerang effect, which often comes back rather quickly in conflicts. We must also take into consideration how our values influence how we think about things and those things we think are important. Because we see the world and experience it through our own value system, when someone does not share these same values, it may distort our perceptions of them. This perception is often expressed through the spirit in which we communicate. This spirit is reflected in what we say and how we say it.

Extended/Expanded Self or WEUSI

A way to develop a caring attitude is to see your partner as an extension of yourself. Since we all are connected through spirit to the Divine, and we are an extension of the Divine, our communication with one another should reflect this. This is referred to as the *extended self* (Nobles, 1976), *expanded self* (Karenga, 1999), and *WEUSI* (Asante, 1980; Williams, 1981). In communication the extended or expanded self says, "when I am talking to you, I am talking to myself. I am you and you are me. I should talk to you in the way that I desire to be talked to." In incorporating the expanded self, extended self, or WEUSI in our communication, we develop an attitude that "I" want to communicate in a manner so that "WE"can feel good and strengthened within ourselves and in our relationship. This benefits "US" which includes our children, our families, our communities and our nation. More fundamentally, you can develop a caring attitude by communicating in a way that shows that you honor and respect your partner and that you honor and respect yourself. In order to develop a caring attitude, you might also focus on the three C's of caring.

The Three C's of Caring

The three C's of caring are consideration, concern, and commitment.

- *I consider you* a person of value, worthy of my consideration, since you have been created in the divine image of God.

- *I am concerned about you* and your happiness and well-being, my own happiness and well—being, and the happiness and well-being of our relationship. I am concerned that you are able to meet your needs, wants, goals, and expectations, and I am able to meet mine.

- *I am committed* to you and to this relationship.

Essentially, incorporating the three C's in communicating with your partner helps both of you communicate in ways that honor and respect the other. And honor and respect are necessary to maintain a good relationship.

Talking and Listening with Care

If you recall, effective talk is (a) when body talk and word talk are consistent and (b) the words that are used are constructive. Effective listening is that which is done with care and understanding. To use good talking and listening skills in ways that allow each partner to express him/herself requires that while one is talking, the other listens and reflects back what the other has said. When one is finished expressing him or herself, the other listens and reflects what she/he has said. Talking and reflective listening are quite simple:

When $\boxed{\text{you talk}}$ — I listen with care and reflect back what you have said.

When $\boxed{\text{I talk}}$ — you listen with care and reflect back what I have said.

Although talking and listening with care can become a natural part of communication and can be used with anyone, e.g. co-workers, family members and friends, there are primarily two instances in which TLC is necessary when communicating with your partner. One is when he or her is trying to work through a problem or issue and desires your help. The other is when conflict arises. How to talk and listen with care is outlined in the chapters that follow.

Helping Your Partner Talk Through a Problem Using TLC

There are instances in which your partner may have a problem that he/she wishes to discuss with you. His/her problem may have nothing to do with you. It may have to do with work, family, friends, or a decision about something. In other instances, he/she may need to vent frustration. When we find ourselves in such a situation, our natural response is to help. This leads us to engage in listening and responding that, although the intent is to help, gets in the way.

Carl Rogers, a noted psychologist, found 80 percent of communication between individuals to be evaluative, interpretative, supportive, probing, and understanding, in that order (Johnson, 2000). How do these methods of listening and responding and the roles we assume help and how do they hinder us from helping our partners talk through a problem?

- *Evaluative*—When giving an evaluative response, often the individual assumes the role of an advisor. Advising can be helpful in some circumstances, and people may even ask for it in others. However, giving advice can be threatening, putting the individual on the defense, particularly when he/she is just seeking to express his/her thoughts and feelings for understanding. When telling your partner what he/she ought to do, you are making the assumption that he/she does not already know what to do. It can also be perceived that you are being judgmental, because it may indicate that your partner has failed at or is not doing something he/she should be doing. It can also suggest that you know more about the issue than your partner, with the ultimate effect of making him/her feel inferior.

- *Interpretive*—When giving an interpretive response, many of us assume the role of therapist. Although many people need psychotherapy, there are professionals for this and a time and place for it. When you assume the role of therapist, you may start telling your partner what his/her problem means, his/her motivations behind it, what is really going on with him/her. This may communicate to your partner that you know more about him/her or his/her motivations than he/she knows. The interpretive response can also be threatening and put your partner on the defense.

- *Supportive*—Although for many of us, our intention is to be supportive of our partner, when he/she is experiencing a problem, what often happens is we end up minimizing what he/she is feeling. This happens when trying to be supportive, you say things that seem to indicate that you lack interest, understanding, or empathy. For example, your partner might express that he/she feels bad or hurt about something and you make statements like, "That's life," or "You got to take the bitter with the sweet." You may also minimize your partner's feelings when trying to talk him/her out of how he/she is feeling by making statements like, "You need to snap out of it," "You need to get over it and move on." These kinds of responses have the ultimate effect of saying to your partner, "You should not feel the way you are feeling." As with the others, these responses, can be threatening, and even hurtful.

■ *Probing*—Although asking questions can make your partner feel that you are interested in what he/she is saying and deepen understanding, it can also get in the way of effective communication. If you are going to ask questions for clarity, it is important to ask open-ended questions. This allows your partner more freedom to talk about his/her thoughts and feelings. Also, it is important to not ask "why" questions, because most people cannot tell you the reasons that they do things. It may also make your partner defensive, because asking him/her why he/she did something may communicate disapproval or criticism. Because some "why" questions may put your partner in the position to have to justify his/her decision, it may prohibit him/her from further exploration into his/her thoughts and feelings about the problem.

■ *Understanding* — An understanding listener, listens to his/her partner with care and reflects back what he/she has said. This technique communicates to your partner that you have heard what he/she has said, and that you are trying to understand his/her thoughts and feelings. Thus, rather than asking questions, you can seek clarity through reflecting back what your partner has said. By doing this, you also communicate to your partner that you have heard and understood him/her.

As indicated, all of these communication techniques may be useful at some time or another and can be effective when used under the right circumstances. Also, none of them are good or bad, it is failure to recognize when and when not to use these various listening techniques that interfere with our communication and the building of a quality relationship.

Also, overuse of any of the methods can be a barrier to effective communication. Carl Rogers found that "When a person uses one category of response as much as 40 percent of the time, then others see him as

Helping Your Partner 47

always responding that way" (Johnson, p. 232). In many instances when your partner is talking to you he/she may need you to just listen. In fact, he/she may already have resolved the problem. Caring and understanding listening may be the most effective communication technique in helping your partner work through a problem. By using caring and understanding listening strategies discussed here and the previous chapter, you would simply reflect what your partner has said. Let's take Kenya and Kenyatta, for example.

Kenya expresses:

I am so overweight. I need to go on a diet. I feel so unattractive. Ugh, I can't stand the way I look. It makes me feel bad about myself.

Table 3

Kenyatta's Responses	Impact
Evaluative: I didn't want to say it, but I think you should be concerned about your weight. Maybe you should think about joining the gym.	Although she thinks that she has a weight problem and feels unattractive, she may have not known that he also sees her as unattractive, which make her feel worse.
Interpretive: Your problem is that you are too focused on your physical appearance. Maybe you should get help with your self-esteem instead of your weight.	This statement might put her on the defense. She may now feel compelled to defend his accusation that she is too focused on physical appearance and that she has issues with self-esteem.
Supportive: You should stop feeling bad about your weight and look at the blessings you have.	She should not be feeling the way she does. This statement may undermine how she is feeling.
Probing: Why do you think that you are overweight?	She now has to explain what she is thinking and how she is feeling about her weight.
Understanding: So you think you are overweight. You feel unattractive. Is there any thing I can do to support you or make you feel better? *Or* He could just simply say, "I love you the way you are."	She feels heard, understood, loved, and supported.

By being a caring and understanding listener, Kenyatta has allowed Kenya to talk about what she is thinking and how she is feeling without having to feel guilty about her feelings, answer a lot of questions, defend herself, or be told what is wrong with her. Kenya feels good that she has someone who will listen and understands her. Also, because Kenyatta used caring and understanding listening, it helps Kenya to feel connected to him; therefore, she feels closer to him. This, overall, helps their relationship.

Using the TLC Three-Step Program to Resolve Conflicts

We all have needs, wants, goals and expectations. It is important to distinguish clearly between these:

- *Need* — a condition or situation in which something is necessary
- *Want* — a great desire or a wish for something
- *Goal* — a purpose toward which an endeavor is directed; an objective
- *Expectation* — anticipation of something; to look forward to the probable occurrence or appearance of something

Generally, an issue or problem arises when there is inconsistency between what we need or want and what we are actually getting. Someone or something is interfering with our goals or our expectations about the way things ought to be or the way we would like for things to be. In essence, an issue or problem arises when our wants, needs or goals are not being met or when something or someone falls short of what is anticipated. When this occurs, it may lead to conflict. There are some factors, however, to consider about conflict:

- It is inevitable — To be human is to have conflict. We all have different needs, wants, goals, and expectations at different times. No two people are going to share the same needs, wants, or goals at the same time. Therefore no two people are going to be on the same accord 100 percent of the time. It is how we conflict that makes a difference.

- It may be a blessing — It can be seen as a curse and responded to accordingly or it can be seen as a blessing. A conflict may be a wake-up call, a message from the spirit world, that something is wrong in our lives, or something is going in the wrong direction in our relationship. It may indicate that something needs changing. Conflict may lead individuals take steps to make the changes necessary to preserve the relationship.

- It is necessary because it:

  - Helps us to clarify our own wants, needs, goals, and expectations, and the values underlying them.

  - Helps our partners to clarify their needs, wants, goals, and expectations, and values underlying them.

- Helps us to grow as individuals.

- Helps us to grow together.

- It is how we handle conflict that matters — having communication competencies is needed to resolve conflicts effectively.

- The goal of conflict is to make sure each partner's needs, wants, goals or expectations are met, while simultaneously maintaining the integrity of the relationship.

Factors to Consider About Issues/Problems

- There are problems that can be resolved and some that cannot. It is estimated that close to 70 percent of problems cannot be solved. Typically, those problems stem from differences in world view and/or values.

- It is important to distinguish between those problems that can be resolved and those that cannot. To do this, it is important to see whether the issue stems from differences in world view or values or it whether it has to do with power struggles, habitual behavior or simply logistics. If it has to do with habitual behavior, or logistics, then you would focus on strategies to re-work the logistics or change the behavior. If it is about power, both partners would focus on compromising. If a conflict evolves around differences in world view or values, it is important to come to some resolve on how to respect each other's differences and develop strategies on how to co-exist with them.

■ The focus should center on solving those problems or issues that can be resolved.

Offensive and Defensive Talk

Conflict resolution consists of trying to resolve a problem or come to some resolution about an issue. Often, however, in trying to resolve conflict, many do so by engaging in talk that is offensive and defensive.

■ *Offensive Talk* — Although the intent may not be to offend, individuals often have few skills to express their discontent or dissatisfaction that their needs, wants, goals, or expectations are not being met. This dissatisfaction combined with lack of effective communication skills can lead them to communicate in ways that can be offensive. Other times, because the person has felt disregarded or disrespected in some way, they do intend to offend. The individual wants the other person to feel or experience what they are feeling or experiencing. They therefore communicate by lashing out. In lashing out, they may hurt, wound, or inflict the same pain that they perceive that the other individual is causing. In doing this, they may also show disrespect or disregard. When one communicates in this manner, he or she typically puts the other individual on the defense.

■ *Defensive Talk* — An individual who communicates in an offensive mode may trigger the other person to go into a defensive mode. This defensive mode protects the other person from words that wound or hurt. The other person may also go into an offensive mode by lashing back at the offensive person in an attempt to wound or hurt back. Alternatively, the defender may just shut down emotionally to ward off attacks and say nothing.

Using offensive-defensive talk, neither of the parties are listening; both are talking to defend their respective positions or themselves from attacks by the other. By resorting to this form of communication, they get nowhere. In offensive-defensive talk, one or both parties get hurt. The objective is to get to a place where you can resolve conflicts in a way that is respectful and where the needs, wants, goals, desires, or expectations of both parties can be met.

Conflict Styles

There are generally three styles that couples can use to resolve conflict, all of which may have positive and negative consequences. As shown in *Table 4*, one or both partners may seek to resolve a problem, but because they lack communication skills it leads to misunderstandings. Also, because one or the other both lack communication skills, neither may hear the other, and therefore neither may get a chance to hear the other's point of view and/or why the other may be thinking and feeling the way he/she does. Because both may also talk at the same time and each is trying to get his/her point across without listening to the other, the situation may escalate and get out of control. With this conflict resolution style, in some instances the issue or problem may get resolved; in others, it may not.

If both partners seek to resolve the issue and have communication skills or competencies, they may be able to come to some resolution in a manner that both feel heard, understood, respected and the relationship is left intact.

Table 4

Conflict Style	Both Seek to Resolve Conflict	Neither Seeks to Resolve Conflict	One Seeks to Resolve Conflict, While Other Seeks to Avoid it
Outcomes			
Positive	Using skills can lead to healthy resolution.	Live with it and just move on.	
Negative	Without skills, can lead to misunderstandings; may be resolved or left un-resolved.	Can lead to build-up of resentment, and eventually, emotional distance.	Breeds frustration, resentment, negative perceptions and eventual emotional distance

In some instances, neither partner may seek to resolve problems or issues. Some couples resort to this when they find that they are unable to resolve problems without things escalating and getting out of control. For others, this method may work best for them. They may leave the issue unresolved and just move on and they may be able to continue a healthy relationship. On the other hand, avoiding conflict may lead to a build-up of resentment on the part of one or both partners. This may lead one or both to become emotionally distant.

If one partner seeks to resolve problems while the other seeks to avoid them, this may breed frustration on the part of the one who wants to resolve them. He/ she may become resentful and subsequently emotionally distant. When either partner begins to disengage from the other emotionally, it may eventually lead to dissolution of the relationship.

TLC— Three-Step Program

Working through differences or resolving conflicts using TLC include three steps: (1) Inner Talk, (2) Outer Talk, and (3) Co-action.

1. *Inner Talk* begins with going inside yourself to think about the problem first. What you want to do is: (a) be clear on what is causing the problem or issue, (b) identify exactly what the problem/issue is, (c) work through your thoughts, (d) work through your feeling, and (e) make a decision about what to do.

    A. *What is causing the problem/issue?* It is important to identify what happened or did not happen that caused the problem/issue to emerge. What has occurred or what has not occurred to bring about the problem or issue? What need, want, goal or expectation was not met? Be clear and specific about this.

B. *What is the problem or issue?* After identifying what has caused the problem, the next step is to clearly identify what the problem itself is. It is important to name it, to state clearly through inner talk what the issue is.

Questions to Consider

- Your interpretation—Is it as bad as it appears? Does something need to change or do you need to change your perceptions?

- Are there things in your past that might be distorting your perceptions?

- What are the underlying factors?

- If it is something that someone is or is not doing what do you think is motivating it? Is the person aware of it? What might the individual be experiencing that you are not aware of?

- If the individual is aware of it, what might be motivating it?

C. *What are your thoughts?* In working through your thoughts, it is important to differentiate how your focus can influence your perceptions. There are two types of focus you can take in thinking about and ultimately approaching an issue.

Take Dan and Regina for instance. Regina is frustrated because Dan does not fold up clothes after he washes them. They have had numerous discussions about it. After each discussion Dan will then fold up the clothes. But over time, he goes back to his usual way of doing things. Regina's need is for Dan to help fold the clothes so that the house is organized. Her goal is for a neat and more organized environment. Regina's expectation is that Dan will follow through on what he says he will do.

- *Other focus* means you focus on the other person. You focus on your thoughts and feelings about the other person. As it concerns Dan, Regina might think he is sloppy and inconsiderate. This could lead her to communicate in a manner that blames, criticizes, or judges, which means that she may attack him rather than address his behavior.

- *Self-focus* means you focus on yourself, which may include how you are being affected by the problem. Regina may think: "It is hard for me to live in an unorganized environment. My need or want is to have an organized environment. Is there an alternative way to deal with the clothes not being folded. How can I help him help me?"

Here it is important to distinguish clearly between a need and a want. As indicated previously, a need is something that is necessary. In most instances one may have a difficult time living without it. A want is a desire or wish for something. Because wants are often thought to be needs, this may influence one's perception of the issue or problem, which may also affect one's approach to a resolution. If a want is perceived as a need, individuals may feel they cannot live without what it is that is desired. They may, therefore, become entrenched in their position. This entrenchment can lead to unnecessary power struggles, which can ultimately lead to a break in the relationship. Therefore, it is important to distinguish clearly between a need and a want.

By focusing on herself, which means examining her own thoughts, Regina is able to think about her own perceptions and how she can help resolve the issue. If she were to focus on Dan, the approach to take would be to try understand what is motivating his behavior. Is it that it is just a habit that is hard to break? Is it that he does not have enough time to fold the clothes? Is it that it is something that is not important to him, or is he just not considering her? Whatever it might be, the question for Regina is: how do I approach him about the issue?

D. *What are your feelings?* Feelings stem from the kind of emotions the issue evokes. Six major emotions include anger, fear, disgust, sadness, surprise, and happiness. You may also experience variations of these emotions or feelings. Emotions and feelings are physiological reactions to our experiences. For example, anger may evoke physiological changes, such as a more rapid heart rate, the rise of adrenaline in the blood, and increased blood pressure. Such a physiological response might trigger a fight or flight response. Although it is natural to have feelings, and they are a natural response to our experiences, many of us are not adept at expressing them. This may stem from the cultural normative that exists in American society where being emotional is associated with being weak. Expressing emotions and feelings may be especially difficult for some men, since men are not supposed to be weak.

Being self-focused instead of other-focused is also necessary when working through one's feelings. With regard to Regina and Dan, a question Regina might ask herself is, *"What am I feeling?"*

> *Self-focus*—I am feeling overburdened with responsibilities. I am feeling angry because an unorganized environment detracts from my productivity and emotional and spiritual well-being. I am feeling hurt because it seems that he is not considering me.

> *Other-focus*—He is not considering me or the effect an unorganized environment is having on me. He is unorganized. He is inconsiderate. He is a slob.

Even if Regina were to use other-focus, "I" statements could be used. When using "I" statements, she might say: "I feel that I am not being considered," or "I feel unhappy because our environment is disorganized." By using I statements, she is not attacking, blaming or accusing.

Once you have worked through your feelings, the next step is to decide what course of action to take. However, before taking action, you might consider that feelings evoke certain physiological responses; they lead us to naturally want to take action. All emotions produce some type of physiological response. To avoid dealing with feelings may lead one to be physically, emotionally, psychologically, and spiritually un-healthy. Repressing emotions like anger can lead one to experience a host of physical problems stemming from too much adrenaline in the body over a long period of time. Other repressed emotions can lead to a negative outlook on life, make one sick–toxic, someone people don't want to be around. Toxic emotion is like toxic waste—no one wants it in their backyard. Being sick from repressed emotions detracts from our emotional and psychological health, and subsequently our spiritual health, all of which can deprive us of the happiness necessary to lead a satisfying life. Also, not expressing feelings can lead to relationship deterioration because it can:

- Build up resentments, which increase conflict and erects invisible walls between partners. One or both may then seek to emotionally distance him/herself from the relationship;

- Distort perceptions, where words and behaviors of partners are interpreted more negatively, even when the intent is good;

- Prohibit productive relationship work, which includes resolution of relationship problems.

It is, therefore, important to develop skills necessary to express feelings.

As indicated, when an experience brings about an emotion or feeling, it is natural for the body to seek to restore balance. The experiences or sensory perceptions that give rise to our emotions or feelings urge us to take action. The next step, then, is to take action.

    E. *What action will you take?* At this point, you will decide whether to (a) let the problem/issue go or (b) approach your partner so that you can discuss the issue/problem. An important fact to note about inner talk is that you may do it not only while you are awake, but while you are asleep. Sometimes a person may sleep on a problem and by the next day, become more clear about it. What may happen in some instances is that your mind continues to work on the problem subconsciously. Also, among African people, it is believed that a person's spirit visits the spirit world while the person is asleep to seek answers, and that ancestors and other spiritual beings provide help. Thus, when the person awakens, the answer is clear.

By using inner talk and the guidance of the spirit world to help you process and sort through your thoughts and feelings about an issue, you may resolve it yourself, or you may decide that it is not as big a deal as you originally thought it was. You may, therefore, have no need to consider it further. If, on the other hand, you find that it is a problem that you cannot work out by yourself, you may decide that you need to discuss it further with your partner. If you decide you need to talk about it, then the next step is outer talk.

2. ***Outer Talk*** consists of (a) approaching your partner in a respectful manner, (b) planning to work through the issue, (c) Issue Talking and Listening with Care (ITLC), (d) Resolution Talking and Listening with Care (RTLC).

   A. *Approaching your partner*—Factors to consider when approaching your partner include:

   ● Hard approach vs. soft approach—A hard approach is one in which you attack, blame or, accuse, disapprove of or command your partner. A soft approach is when you do not attack, blame or accuse, disapprove of or command your partner. You do not want to be offensive; otherwise it will put your partner in a defensive mode. This can potentially turn the talk into an offensive-defensive match and nothing gets resolved.

- Your emotional state — Are you too emotional or heated about the problem to be able to approach your partner in a way that would avoid hurting his/her feelings or putting him/her on the defense?

- Timing — Is this the right time to bring up the problem or issue or might another time be more appropriate? Is it late at night when your partner is too tired to be receptive to you?

- Difficulties your partner is currently undergoing — What types of issues might he/she be experiencing that could prohibit him/her from being receptive to your approach in a positive way?

B. *Plan to Meet* — Here you and your partner will come to an agreement on a date and time to meet to talk about the issue. You and your partner should decide whether you will discuss it at the time the issue is brought up, or whether another time would be better. It is important to set a date and time that works for both of you.

C. *Issue Talking and Listening with Care (ITLC)*—Using the talking and listening with care skills, talk through the problem. Remember:

When

You talk —I listen with care and reflect back what you say.

When

I talk —You listen with care and reflect back what I say.

Talk and listen with care remembering that you consider your partner, you are concerned that his/her needs, wants, goals, or expectations are met as well as your own and that you are committed to the relationship. Continue to talk and listen, taking turns until you both have thoroughly shared your thoughts and feelings about the specific issue or problem. Make sure you both have said everything you need to say, and have heard and understood everything the other had to say.

Talking Strategies

● Use "I" statements vs. "You" statements—When using "You" statements, the listener might take it as blaming. This may put him/her on the defense. Once in the defense mode, the individual is now in the position to block out what you are saying, making it difficult for you to be heard. For example, saying "I feel unloved" vs. "You don't love me," does not blame your partner.

- The Extended Self means "I" am also "You." The objective here is to become your partner. Try to see the world from his/her vantage point. Talk to him/her in a way that you would like to be talked to. Do not offend or hurt.

- Focus on your partner's behavior rather than him or her. Be careful not to make attacks on your partner's personhood, by name calling, belittling, criticizing, or judging; accusing or blaming; questioning his or her trustworthiness; disproving of or showing contempt or disgust; or commanding. People typically will not respond positively if they perceive that an affront is being made to their personhood. Rather than deal with the issue, they will attempt to defend themselves.

- Stay on the subject; be careful to not to stray off to extraneous subjects that have nothing to do with the subject at hand.

- Do not bring up past issues, especially if they are not relevant to the problem at hand.

- Do not argue over facts. Instead of saying, "You said you would. . . " say, "It is my understanding that you would. . ."

- Avoid statements like "always" and "never." These statements might lead your partner to focus on the fact that they do not "always" or "never" do something, rather than the real issue.

- Listen for and outline underlying issues that were not so apparent. Decipher and break down the issue(s) and resolve them one by one. You may decide to talk through the underlying issues during the current discussion, or you might decide to meet at another time to talk through issues that have emerged.

Listening Strategies

- *Focus on the Extended Self*—This entails trying to understand the thoughts and feelings of your partner. By focusing on the extended self, you become him/her. Becoming your partner helps you to understand what he/she may be experiencing or going through. It also helps you to see the world from his/her vantage point. If your partner feels you care enough to consider what he/she is thinking and how she/he is feeling, and that you are trying to see things from his/her point of view, it makes him/her feel more comfortable with talking to you.

- *Paraphrasing*—Essentially you should rephrase what your partner has said or what you think he/she is trying to say. Sometimes it may be good to repeat what he or she has said. Other times, it may be good to use some of the words he/she has said, but not every word. In these instances, you should rephrase your partner's words in your own words. Be sure the content and meaning are consistent with what he or she has said.

Take Dan and Regina again.

Regina says:

"*I really don't think it is fair that the clothes are left for me to fold most of the time.* "

Dan's response might be:

"So what you're saying is that you do not think it is fair that you have to fold the clothes most of the time."

Or

"You think it is unfair that the clothes are left for you to fold most of the time."

Or

"You think I do not do my share of folding the clothes and this is unfair to you."

- *Reflecting Feelings* — Just as it is important to rephrase what your partner has said, it is also important to reflect what you feel she/he is feeling. To reflect what your partner is feeling involves the extended self. You want to think about how you would feel if you were in his/her position. To show that you can feel what your partner is feeling requires having and showing empathy. In reflecting how you feel your partner is feeling, it is important to reflect the depth of what he/she has said and that you understand the meaning behind what was said. Some examples include:

"So you feel hurt that I. . . "

"You feel disappointed by. . ."

"This makes you feel..."

D.   *Resolution Talking and Listening with Care (RTLC)* — Using RTLC both parties participate in generating possible resolutions. There are several steps you can take to reach a resolution.

1. Both partners work together to arrive at possible resolutions, while one might put these ideas on paper.

2. Each partner decides which resolutions they cannot live with. They will then eliminate these from the list.

3. Each partner then decides on the resolutions they can live with.

4. Partners then select the resolutions they can live with. It is important at this step to find common ground. Review the list and circle those solutions that you both agree are possible, selecting at least three. Here it is important for both of you to come to a

resolution by compromising; giving something to receive something.

5. Select the resolution that is the best fit for both of you.

Checklist for Solutions

Donald Knox and Caroline Schacht (2001) identify five questions to consider in generating resolutions. These include:

- Is the resolution mutually satisfying for both of you?

- Is the resolution specific? Are both of you clear on what you are to do, when, where, and how?

- Is the resolution realistic? Can both of you achieve what you have proposed?

- Have you specified what you will do if the problem or issue recurs?

- What strategies have you included to prevent the problem or issue from recurring? (p. 223)

3. *Co-action* includes acting together to do the following:

A. Initiate and carry out the resolution—You will actually implement the resolution. It is important that both you remain committed to what you said you would do.

B. Meet again to evaluate the outcome—You want to find out whether you have been willing and able to follow through on the resolution, and whether the desired results have been achieved.

Factors to Consider

● Things might not turn out the way you expect. Often our plans seem achievable in the ideal but are not realistic.

● Old habits die hard; it is important to incorporate strategies to help both of you get back on track should one or both of you fail to follow through on your part of the agreement. This is particularly the case when the resolution involves breaking a habit. To do this you may include ways in which you will remind each other, for example, reminder notes, a gesture, or a statement when one forgets.

Examples:

A tap on the knee—This is a strategy a couple used every time one would begin a discussion about a topic which the other thought was too personal or embarrassing in front of friends. One partner would just tap the other on the knee.

Sticky notes—These were used in another instance when a partner would forget to pick up his socks.

A penny for your thoughts—This was an expression used by a couple when the other felt one was too quiet or felt shut-out or alone. Essentially, when she desired his attention or conversation from him, she would pass him a penny.

Whatever strategies you use to help break old habits, these should be agreed upon by both of you beforehand. Even though you agree on strategies, each should be responsible for changing his/her habits. If there is a need to revise the strategies, you should use TLC.

● You may have to revisit the plan; if you find that you have to revisit the plan, repeat the ITLC and RTLC steps under the TLC three-step program.

In conclusion, communication is essential to our survival. TLC includes communication competencies in talking, listening, and showing a caring attitude. Effective talking includes using constructive word and body talk and being sure they are consistent. Effective listening is listening with care and understanding. It means filtering out negative perceptions so that these perceptions are not reflected in your attitude. Showing a caring attitude includes focusing on the three C's, consideration for your partner, showing that you are concerned that his/her needs, wants, and goals are met as well as your own, and showing commitment to the relationship. The TLC three-step program includes working through inner talk (one's thoughts and feelings), outer talk (using strategies to approach your partner, ITLC, and RTLC), and co-action (moving together to carry out your resolution). By developing understanding of how to communicate effectively and developing competencies in these areas, partners can work through their individual issues, solve problems they share mutually, and look forward to a lasting relationship.

When you and your partner are able to navigate through lower levels of communication, solving problems that are individually or mutually shared, you can spend more time and energy on higher levels of communication—that which is mutually expansive. Exchanging ideas helps you and your partner to merge and become one. Expansive communication is the key to spiritual growth and spiritual growth is the key to a satisfying and fulfilling life together. With good communication skills, more energy and time can be devoted to bringing good, doing good, and carrying out your divine purpose. These indeed, are necessary for eternity in the afterlife.

Communication Exercises

Following are exercises to help you and your partner increase your awareness of your individual communication styles, the source of these styles, and how you communicate and resolve conflict.

Series 1 Exercises: Parental/Caregivers Communication and Conflict Styles

These questions are designed to help you look at how your parents communicated and to ascertain your thoughts and feelings about it. Answer the questions by writing in your response.

1. Describe how your parents (caregivers) communicated with each other and to you and your siblings.

_____

_____

_____

_____

_____

2. Which best characterizes how your parents resolved conflicts and what their relationship was like.

❏ They argued passionately. They, however, were still able to resolve their conflicts and had a warm and loving relationship.

❏ They discussed issues in a controlled and calm manner. They disagreed, but agreed to disagree. They generally let each other know their opinion but did so respectfully. They validated each other and showed that they valued each other's opinions. They had a good relationship.

❏ One parent would argue, dominating the conversation, while the other parent would say little or nothing, tune him/her out or just leave. Their relationship was emotionally distant, and they seemed to live separate lives.

❏ They engaged in offensive and defensive arguments where they would talk at the same time, one or the other yelling. One or both of them would attack the other, blame, call names, accuse and/or belittle. Their relationship was distant, and they really did not have much to say to each other at times. They spent very little time together.

When a problem or issue emerged, neither sought to discuss it. They just believed that it would eventually work itself out or that if you pray on it, it would resolve itself. They still had a loving and caring relationship.

❏ I was raised by one caregiver. This does not apply to me.

❏ Other–describe how your parents resolved conflicts.

_____

_____

_____

_____

_____

3. What do you *think* about how your parents communicated and discussed issues?

_____

_____

_____

_____

_____

4. How do you *feel* about how your parents communicated and resolved conflicts?

_____

_____

_____

_____

_____

5. In comparison to your own parents (caregivers), how did your *partner's* parents (caregivers) communicate and resolve conflicts?

_____

_____

_____

_____

Series 2 Exercises: You and Your Partner's Communication, Processing and Conflict Resolution Styles

These exercises are designed to help you and your partner determine how your styles of communicating and discussing issues may have been influenced by your parents/caregivers. They are also designed for you and your partner to take a closer look at how both of you communicate, process your thoughts and feelings, and resolve issues or problems.

1. How is your style of communicating with your partner similar to or different from your parents' style of communication?

_____

_____

_____

_____

_____

2. What impact do you think your parents' style of communicating and resolving conflict has had on your own style?

_____

_____

_____

_____

_____

3. How is your partner's style of communication similar to or different from his/her parents?

_____

_____

_____

_____

_____

4. Describe how you think your partner's parents' communication style has influenced his/her communication and conflict-resolution style.

_____

_____

_____

_____

_____

5. *Instructions:* For the questionnaire that follows, first answer the questions as they apply to you. After you have completed it, you should then answer the questions according to how you think your partner communicates. Your partner should do the same. First, he/she should answer the questions for himself. Then he/she should answer the questions according to how he/she thinks you communicate. You should then proceed on to the next questionnaire before discussion.

When communicating, how often do you/your partner do the following:	Very little				Very Often
	1	2	3	4	5
1. Speak for others by putting words in their mouth.	1	2	3	4	5
2. Wait until the individual finishes talking before you speak.	1	2	3	4	5
3. Interrupt when others are talking.	1	2	3	4	5
4. Reflect what the person is saying so that he/she is sure your heard him/her.	1	2	3	4	5
5. Try to understand and see the other person's point of view.	1	2	3	4	5
6. Lose control and start yelling by blaming, attacking, accusing, and/or belittling the person .	1	2	3	4	5
7. Say anything possible to get the person to see things your way.	1	2	3	4	5
8. Get upset if the person does not see things your way.	1	2	3	4	5
9. Make sarcastic and undercutting remarks.	1	2	3	4	5

If you circled very often, numbers 4 or 5 for questions 1, 3, 6, 7, 8 and 9 in the previous questionnaire, these may be areas that you or your partner need to work on.

6. *Instructions:* For the questions that follow, check the response which applies to what you wish your partner would do, were more like, or had. Your partner should also do the same. After you both have completed your answers, you should then discuss your styles of communicating with each other. After you have done this, for questions 7-10, write how you would like to change your communication and how you would like your partner to change his/hers. You should also list how your partner would like to change his/her communication style and the changes your partner would like you to make. In your discussion, you may address each problem area separately, or you may address them together. The four primary problem areas include:

- Talking Style — the manner in which your partner talks to you.

- Listening Style — the manner in which your partner listens to you.

- Processing Style—the way your partner processes his/her thoughts and feelings.

- Sensitivities—how sensitive your partner is to things you say, even when the intent is good. Some people are more sensitive than others and may not take kindly to things said by others, even if they are said with good intent or in humor.

Strategies you could use to discuss communication, processing and conflict resolution styles might include: (a) discussing the primary areas listed above at different times or (b) one partner discuss his/her issues at one time and the other partner discuss his/her issues at another time. Whatever strategy you use, it is important to use TLC.

6. I wish my partner were/would/had:

❏ talk to me more	❏ stay on the subject when discussing issues	❏ stop saying offensive and hurtful things
❏ not so sensitive to things I say	❏ more of a sense of humor	❏ not take things so personally

❏ more open with his/her feelings

❏ listen to me more

❏ not cut me off when I am talking

❏ value my advice

❏ respect my opinion more

❏ not avoid discussing issues

❏ appreciate my sense of humor

❏ stop attacking me, by calling me names and putting me down

❏ stop blaming and accusing me of things

❏ stop acting like he/she is disgusted by me

❏ stop trying to boss me around

❏ stop holding things in and talk about them

❏ stop putting our business out, e.g. telling people about our personal affairs

❏ work on his/her attitude and body language

❏ stop acting like he/she is irritated by me

Other things not listed above that bother me about how my partner communicates include:

a._____

b._____

c._____

d._____

7. Things I would like to change about how I communicate:

a._____

b._____

c._____

d._____

8. Things I would like to change about how my partner communicates:

a._____

b._____

c._____

d._____

9. Things my partner would like to change about how he/she communicates:

a._____

b._____

c._____

d._____

10. Things my partner would like to change about how I communicate:

a._____

b._____

c._____

d._____

Processing Styles

For the questions that follow, circle the number that corresponds to how often this method is used to work through your thoughts and feelings when a problem or issue arises. Then decide whether you and your partner have different or similar processing styles. If you have different ways in which you process problems or issues, you should discuss how each of you respond to the way you process and how you feel about it. Following this, discuss and then write down strategies to help you deal with each other's processing styles.

When an issue or problem arises I usually:	Not Often			Very Often	
	1	2	3	4	5
1. Talk about it with my family members, friends, or someone other than my partner first.	1	2	3	4	5
2. Pray and really think about it before I talk about it with my partner.	1	2	3	4	5
3. Do not like to talk about it until I figure out what to do.	1	2	3	4	5
4. Talk about it with my partner as soon as it emerges.	1	2	3	4	5
5. Spend a lot of time thinking about it first before talking to my partner.	1	2	3	4	5
6. Do something to forget about the problem or issue, hoping it will just go away.	1	2	3	4	5

7. Need space to reflect on my
   thoughts and feelings.   1 2 3 4 5

8. Don't bother with or think
   about issues.   1 2 3 4 5

9. Just let the problem work itself
   out.   1 2 3 4 5

If you or your partner have a score of 4 or 5 for questions 1, 3, and 7 above, you may be an internal processor. If you or your partner have a score of 4 or 5 for questions 1, 4, and 5 you may be an external processor. If either of you have a score of 4 or above for questions 6, 8, and 9, you might avoid working through your thoughts and feelings about problems. If your scores are below 3 for questions in different categories, you might process some things internally and other things externally, while for others you may avoid.

1. If a problem or issue arises, I usually:

_____

_____

_____

2. If a problem or issue arises, my partner usually:

_____

_____

_____

3. If your and your partner's processing styles are different, how do you (a) feel about it, and (b) usually respond to it?

_____

_____

_____

4. How does your partner (a) feel about it and (b) usually respond to it?

_____

_____

_____

5. If you do not feel good about your different processing styles, list strategies that could be used to help you and/or your partner feel better about it.

a._____

b._____

c._____

d._____

Conflict Resolution

The questions below ask you to respond to how you resolve conflicts and how you feel about it. After completing the questions, you should discuss them and then outline how you both would like to change your approach to resolving conflicts.

1. Which best characterizes the way you and your partner resolve conflicts?

❏ We argue passionately. We, however, still respect each other, are still able to resolve our problems, and have a warm and loving relationship.

❏ We discuss issues in a controlled and calm manner. We disagree, but agree to disagree. We generally let each other know our opinion but do so respectfully. We validate each other and show that we value and respect each other's opinions.

❏ One of us do most of the talking, essentially dominating the conversation, while the other says little or nothing, tunes the other out or just leaves. Our relationship is distant and is becoming even more distant. We might be heading down a path of separate lives, or we might eventually break up.

❏ We engage in offensive and defensive arguments where we talk at the same time and one or the other yells. One or both of us attacks the other, blames, calls the other names and/or puts the other down. Our relationship is distant, and we really do not have much to say to each other at times. We spend very little time together.

❏ When a problem emerges, neither of us seeks to discuss it and this is acceptable to us. We believe that things will eventually work themselves out. One or both of us may believe that if we turn it over to God, He will take care of it. We still have a loving and caring relationship.

2. *Instructions*: For the following questions, answer according to what you thought and felt about an argument you had recently with your partner, and/or one in which the communication either got out of control or was unproductive. Follow these steps: (a) identify what the problem was, (b) fill out the questionnaire that follows indicating how it made you feel, (c) write down the role you played in why the communication turned out the way it did, (d) discuss it with your partner. In your discussion, make sure that you both check to see if you share the same perception of the problem. Having different ideas about what the problem is often underlies why it is difficult to resolve.

The argument that we had about *(name it)*_____

_____

focused on

_____

_____

When we discussed this issue, I felt	Not at all						A lot
	1	2	3	4	5	6	7
Disrespected	1	2	3	4	5	6	7
Disregarded	1	2	3	4	5	6	7
Hurt	1	2	3	4	5	6	7
Sad	1	2	3	4	5	6	7
Angry	1	2	3	4	5	6	7
Disgusted	1	2	3	4	5	6	7
Misunderstood	1	2	3	4	5	6	7
Anxious/Worried	1	2	3	4	5	6	7
Belittled	1	2	3	4	5	6	7
Invalidated	1	2	3	4	5	6	7
Criticized	1	2	3	4	5	6	7
Blamed	1	2	3	4	5	6	7
Accused	1	2	3	4	5	6	7
Unappreciated	1	2	3	4	5	6	7
Rejected	1	2	3	4	5	6	7

The role I played in how the communication turned out
(What I did or did not do).

_____

_____

3. *Instructions*: Circle *True* or *False* for the questions below based on how you feel when having a discussion with your partner. Your partner should also do the same. For those responses in which the answer is true, this may indicate that work needs to be done in this area.

When communicating with my partner, I generally:	True (T)	False (F)
1. Don't feel heard.	T	F
2. Feel misunderstood.	T	F
3. Don't feel that my partner considers what I have to say.	T	F
4. Don't think my partner thinks what I have to say is important.	T	F
5. Feel ignored by my partner.	T	F
6. Feel that I cannot disagree without things getting out of control.	T	F
7. Feel like I am being controlled.	T	F
8. Feel like I'm being punished if I do not agree .	T	F

3. Overall, what do you *think* about how you and your partner resolve issues?

_____

_____

_____

_____

_____

4. How do you *feel* about how you and your partner resolve problems?

_____

_____

_____

_____

_____

5. Things you would like to change about how you and your partner resolve issues:

_____

_____

_____

_____

_____

6. Strategies you and your partner might use to help resolve issues in a more healthy manner:

a. _____

b. _____

c. _____

d. _____

Series 3 Exercises: Helping Your Partner Talk Through an Issue

For the cases below, write in a caring listener response. Then compare your response to the different listening responses which include evaluative, interpretative, supportive, and probing responses as discussed in chapter three.

1. I don't feel like going to that job. I feel like they want too much from me. Sometimes it feels like they want blood. This job really stresses me out.

   A caring response:

2. I really like talking to my brother because our conversations are on a higher level. But I just get tired of him asking me for money. Almost every time I talk to him, he asks me for money.

   A caring response:

3. I am feeling really depressed and out of it.
Sometimes I wonder why I am even here.

A caring response:

Series 4 Exercises : Talking and Listening Skills

Changing a Hard Approach to a Soft Approach

For each statement below, change the hard approach
to a soft approach. Be sure to use "I" statements rather
than "You" statements. Also take notice of the use of
words like "always" and "never," and eliminate them
from your revised statements.

1. Tanya is frustrated because Charles will not clean the bathroom. He also will not clean the tub after he uses it. Before she gets into the tub, she either has to clean it or get into a dirty tub.

Hard Approach: You never clean up the bathroom after yourself. I'm sick and tired of this! This tub is disgusting! I can't take this anymore!

What is wrong with this statement?

Soft Approach:

2. Justin is frustrated because he does not have sex with Twyla as frequently as he would like. He even thinks that she comes to bed in unattractive pajamas to keep from enticing him.

Hard Approach: Why do you come to bed with those ugly pajamas on? Before we got married you used to wear sexy lingerie all the time. Now all you wear are those pajamas. What's up with that? If you don't want to have sex, just say it. You don't have to come to bed looking like that.

What is wrong with this statement?

Soft Approach:

3. Dequanna is upset because Jawanza does not call her when he says he will. He will say, "I'll call you tonight," but might not call until the next day. This is upsetting to her because she awaits his call. Because there are others who are interested in her, she is even considering leaving the relationship.

Hard Approach: You never call when you say will. Then I am sitting around waiting for you. I could be doing something else. In fact, I even have people who are interested in me. I don't have to be sitting around waiting for you.

What is wrong with this statement?

Soft Approach:

4. Patty is upset because Mark has difficulty budgeting money and spends all the time. She is afraid that his spending habits will lead them to financial ruin.

Hard Approach: You are messing up our lives with the way you spend money. You are so irresponsible. If you keep spending like this, you are going to ruin us. You need to get your act together.

What is wrong with this statement?

Soft Approach

Changing "You" statements to "I" statements:

First change the "You" statements to "I" statements. Then assume the role of listener and paraphrase the statement in a positive manner.

1. You are so sloppy. You never hang up your clothes. I am sick and tired of picking up after you.

Change to "I" statements

Paraphrased statement

2. You always leave dishes in the sink and on the counter. You never wash dishes after you eat. In fact, you don't help wash dishes at all. You always leave that on me.

Change to "I" statements

Paraphrased statement

3. You are always late. You think somebody is going to be sitting around waiting for you. You are four hours late, and I am supposed to be happy that you're here.

Change to "I" statements

Paraphrased statement

4. You never spend time with me. Whenever you are off work you do things without me. All you think about is yourself.

Change to "I" statements

Paraphrased statement

Series 5 Exercises : Resolving an Issue Using the TLC Three-Step Program

Use the TLC Three-Step Program to solve or work through an issue you are currently experiencing.

Step One: Inner Talk

A. **Identify the issue/problem:** Exactly what is the problem?

B. **What caused the problem?** What occurred or did not occur that led to the problem? How did it come about?

C. **Mind Talk:** What are your thoughts?

Self focus: (Focus on your thoughts of how your partner's actions affects you rather than what you think about him/her)

My thoughts are

D. **Heart Talk:** What are your feelings?

Self focus: (Focus on how your partner's actions make you feel rather than how you feel about him/her)

My feelings are

Step Two: Outer Talk

A. Approach your partner

Soft Approach: (*Using a soft approach, construct what you will say when you approach your partner*)

B. **Plan to work through the issue**. However, before approaching your partner, consider whether this is the appropriate time to bring up the problem.

1. My emotional state about the issue is

2. The best time to bring this up is

3. Difficulties my partner are facing now

A better time to bring this up might be

_____

After approaching your partner, you both should agree to a date and time to discuss the problem.

We will meet and discuss the issue on (*date and time*) _____

C. Issue Talking and Listening with Care (ITLC)
1. Identify and describe at least three *talking strategies* you will use:

Partner 1

a._____

b._____

c._____

Partner 2

a._____

b._____

c._____

2. Identify three *listening strategies* you will use:

Partner 1

a._____

b._____

c._____

Partner 2

a._____

b._____

c._____

3. After discussing the issue using TLC, outline the underlying issues that emerged:

a._____

b._____

c._____

We will deal with:

Issue: ❏ Now   ❏ Another
1. _____   time_____

_____

2. _____   ❏ Now   ❏ Another
                   time_____

_____

3._____   ❑ Now ❑ Another
time_____

_____

D. Resolution Talking and Listening with Care (RTLC)

1. Each partner should clearly indicate their needs, wants, goals, and/or expectations in the spaces below. It might not be necessary to fill in all the spaces. Just fill in the ones that apply to you. Also, the issue may be an issue for one partner and not the other. Fill in the spaces as they apply to your situation.

Partner 1

a. My wants are

b. My needs are

c. My goals are

d. My expectations are

Partner 2

a. My wants are

b. My needs are

c. My goals are

d. My expectations are

Possible Resolutions

1. Brainstorming, each partner should write down possible resolutions.

Partner 1

a._____

b._____

c._____

Partner 2

a._____

b._____

c._____

2. Write down those resolutions you *cannot* live with.

Partner 1

a._____

b._____

Partner 2

a._____

b._____

3. Combined possible resolutions:

a._____

b._____

c._____

4. The final solution:

_____

_____

5. Plans *(write down exactly what each party will do)* If only one partner is expected to change their behavior, then fill in his/her one side only.

Partner 1

Will:_____

_____

_____

_____

Date and Time:

_____

Where:_____

_____

How it will be done:

_____

_____

_____

_____

_____

Partner 2

Will: _____

_____

_____

_____

Date and Time:

_____

Where:_____

_____

How it will be done:

_____

_____

_____

_____

_____

6. Possible reminders for behavior change (*put a star by the one you actually use*):

a._____

b._____

c._____

7. Plans if solution needs to be revisited:

a._____

b. _____

c._____

8. Solution Checklist: Check the boxes if your solution meets that criteria. If it does not meet all the criteria below, you may need to revise it. The solution. . .

❏ is mutually beneficial to both of us and the relationship

❏ is specific; we are both clear on what he/she is to do–what, when, where, and how

❏ is realistic; both of us can achieve what we have proposed to do

❏ includes strategies to keep the problem from recurring

❏ includes ways to remind each other of what we are supposed to be doing

Step Three: Co-Action

1. We will begin to implement and carry out this plan starting *(date and time)* _____

2. We will meet again to evaluate our plan on *(date and time)*_____

References

Asante, M.K. (1987). *The Afrocentric idea.* Philadelphia, PA: Temple University Press.

Asante, M.K. (1980). *Afrocentricity: The theory of social change.* Buffalo: Amulefi.

Bâ, A. H. (1981). The living tradition. In J. Ki-Zerbo (Ed.), *General history of Africa Vol. I: Methodology and African prehistory* (pp. 166-203). California: UNESCO.

Curruthers, J. (1995). *Mdw ntr: Divine speech.* Lawrenceville, NJ: Red Sea Press.

Garner, T. (1998). Understanding oral rhetorical practices in African American cultural practices. In V. J. Duncan (Ed.), *Towards achieving MAAT* (pp. 29-44). Dubuque, Iowa: Kendall Hunt.

Gray, J. 1992). *Men are from Mars, women are from Venus.* New York: Harper Collins.

Johnson, D. W. (2000). *Reaching out: Interpersonal effectiveness and self actualization,* 7th edition. Boston: Allyn and Bacon.

Karenga, M. (1999). Sources of self in ancient Egyptian autobiographies. In J.L. Conyers, Jr. (Ed.), *Black American intellectualism and culture: A study of American social and political thought* (pp. 37-57). Stamford, CT: JAI Press.

Karenga, M. (1989). *Selections from the Husia: Sacred wisdom of ancient Egypt.* Los Angeles: The University of Sankore Press.

Knox, D. & Schacht, C. (2002). *Choices in relationships: An introduction to marriage and the family.* 7th ed. Belmont, CA: Wadsworth.

Nobles, W. W. (1976). Extended self: Rethinking the so-called Negro concept. In M. Coleman (Ed.), *Black children just keep on growing* (pp. 160-167). Washington, DC: Black Child Development Institute.

Tannen, D. (1990). *You just don't understand: Women and men in conversation.* New York: Ballantine Books.

Williams, R. (1981). *The collective Black mind: An Afro-centric theory of black personality.* St. Louis, MO: Williams & Associates.

Additional Notes